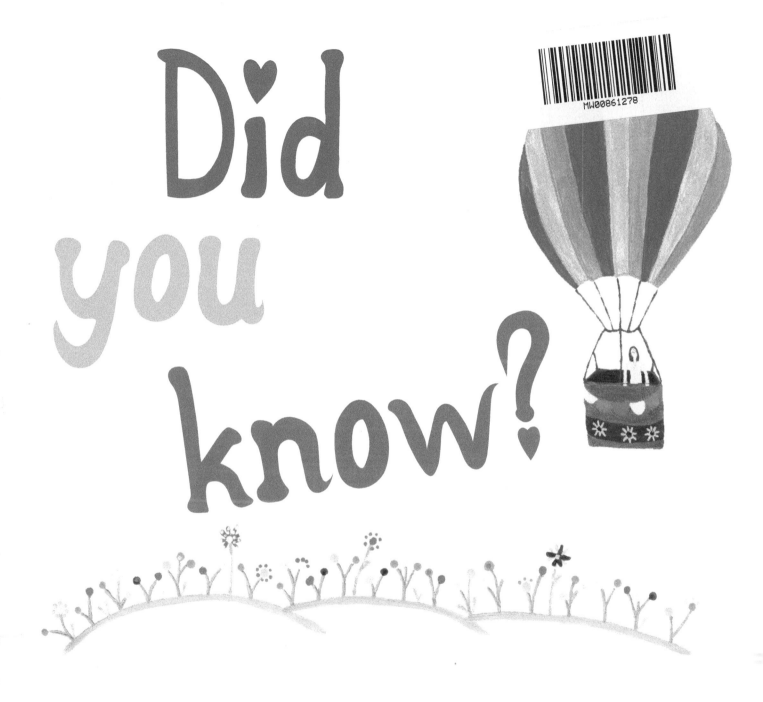

Did you know?

Written by: Marissa Armendariz   Illustrated by: Breanne Burris

Did You Know?

ISBN: 978-1-7354852-4-9

Published by:

narratuscreative | **narratus**press
P.O. Box 1413
Hamilton, OH 45012

Cover design: Breanne Elizabeth Burris
Illustrator: Breanne Elizabeth Burris
Interior Design: **narratus**creative | **narratus**press

Produced in the United States of America

Dedication:

This book is dedicated to my children Aydin, Adaliegh, and Anthony. May you stay resilient, never forget how loved you are, and continue to share your uniqueness with the world.
–Marissa Armendariz

This book is dedicated to my future children. I loved you before I knew you. May this book be an inspiration that dreams do come true. – Breanne Burris

Breanne and Marissa would also like to dedicate this book to the child inside every adult. Regardless of your childhood, may you never be too old to remember and love that small child within you.

Acknowledgments:

Denise Ayers Chaney, we are thankful for the heart you have to share stories. Your kindness and your flexibility in the publishing of this book has not gone unnoticed. We are grateful for Narratus Creative.
- Marissa & Breanne

Rosario Ramirez, thank you for your hard work in the translation of this book to Spanish and for your encouragement. You are appreciated and so deeply valued.
– Marissa & Breanne

Mary Vicario, thank you for all you have taught me about the importance of resiliency, and the difference it makes when individuals are seen and heard. Your teachings and compassion have helped me in healing and have motivated me to pay forward all that you have given to me. – Marissa

My Husband, Jake, I appreciate you being a listening ear and assisting in decision making with the colors of the illustrations. – Breanne

Breanne, thank you for believing in the purpose behind this book so much that you dedicated your time, effort, and money into making sure it reaches the hearts of those it is supposed to reach. – Marissa

Marissa, thank you for the inspiration of the illustrations through your talented writing. – Breanne

Breanne and Marissa met in elementary school. While their upbringing was nearly opposite, they held tightly to each other. They thank God for over 20 years of friendship and His proof that despite any adversity faced, His plans are good.
– Marissa & Breanne

We appreciate the endless encouragement we have received from our loved ones. For every kind word spoken, every prayer prayed, every good intention, we love you.– Marissa & Breanne

About Marissa:

Marissa is a mother of three children; Aydin, Adaliegh, and Anthony (listed oldest to youngest). Her children are full of life and each bring a special touch of rarity to the world around them.

Marissa has always escaped to writing as a place of freedom.

For a short time, Marissa worked in the medical field practicing EKG and Phlebotomy. She has worked in Social Services since 2014 with a focus on Child Development, Mental Health and Homelessness. Marissa has sat on several community boards in an effort to enhance her city. Marissa has a passion to see people be empowered through tough situations. Marissa is a Certified Car Seat Technician, Certified Breastfeeding Counselor, and Certified in Trauma Responsive Care.

Marissa's life experiences, both personally and professionally have allowed her to feel deeply and provide empathy when others are struggling. Despite facing much adversity, she is able to look past the mud and see the flowers so desperately trying to bloom. She enjoys adventure (especially in nature) and believes life is more fun when feet are messy and people are belly laughing.

Marissa believes that family and friendship should be a priority in life. She enjoys styling hair and creating crafts because beauty can be found in anything.

Marissa has a heart for an intimate relationship with Jesus and longs for others to experience His love. She also meets people where they are at in life and is an advocate for inclusion of all races, ages, gender, sexual orientations, classes, religions, and abilities.

When not working or spending time with family and friends, she is dedicating her time to ministry. Marissa understands the impact of community and togetherness.

About Breanne:

Breanne is often referred to as "Bre" by most of her family and friends. She has been married to her husband, Jake, since 2014. As obvious animal lovers, they have five fur babies that consist of two dogs and three cats.

Breanne has a deep desire to be a mother and is hoping to extend her family. She is a natural caretaker as evidenced by her career choice. She is currently a registered nurse on the cardiac unit. Breanne's passion for others pours out of her not only as she works, but any time she interacts with others.

When Breanne sets her mind to a goal, she accomplishes it. Obstacles and challenges may come her way, but she always moves past them.

She has lived in Ohio her whole life. Breanne finds beauty in nature and the simple pleasures in life.

Breanne holds friendship and family close to her heart.

Breanne knows Jesus as her savior, friend, and provider.

Breanne enjoys order and organization, and has also learned to embrace and value the spontaneous moments in life.

Breanne believes in living life with intentional kindness. She loves to turn up the music and sing while in the car, but also partakes in the quietness of watching the sun set.

Breanne enjoys photography, drawing, and painting. She is able to bring words to life. Breanne is loyal to everyone she encounters.

Did you know your laughter
echoes all around?

It is more than just a silly sound.

It carries peace, comfort and joy.

It is more special than your favorite toy.

It's a weapon that fights the deepest sorrows.

It's a gift you have today and for all of your tomorrows.

Did you know that life can
sometimes be unkind?

It pokes and pushes when you just
want to unwind.

But life is a storm, you can dance
in the rain.

You can make positive changes to that beautiful brain.

It's an adventure you can climb any mountain you face.

You get to go at your very own pace.

Did you know there is a difference you can make?

That it is better to give than to take?

You can give your smile, a kind word or three.

You can show the
world how they ought
to be.

A little compassion goes so very far.

Rawrrr

It reaches beyond the sound
of a dinosaur

RAWRRRR!!!

Did you know it is normal to sometimes get scared?

What if you were told there are so many people that care?

Put your hand on your chest, do you feel that beat? That means you have not experienced defeat!

You are a warrior brave and bold. This remains fact, even if you have not been told.

Did you know you may feel emotions you don't want to feel?

Music can help you heal!

You can sing really loud or gentle and sweet.

You can show your best dance moves or sit calmly in your seat.

It is an awesome power to make a choice.

Never forget: YOU have a voice!

Did you know that you are loved more than the stars and the sand?

The love reaches beyond a far-away land.

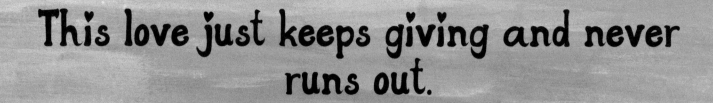

This love just keeps giving and never runs out.

It pulls you away from any self doubt.

You can feel it when you stand next to the ocean and close your eyes.

It always stays, it never says goodbye.

Did you know that with each day there are memories to be made?

Cling to the good ones and
let the bad ones fade.

Watch the sunrise, enjoy
a bubble bath.

Life is a
journey,
choose
your
own
path.

CPSIA information can be obtained
at www.ICGtesting.com
Printed in the USA
BVHW021107230721
612717BV00016B/722